Stewardship

Financial Freedom through Prayer and Obedience

By
Shamika Patrice

"But remember the Lord your God, for it is He who gives
you the ability to produce wealth."
Deuteronomy 8:18

TABLE OF CONTENTS

Dedication

✦   ✦

To my children — *Ma'chir*, *J'aliyah*, and *D'andre* —
you are my greatest blessings and daily reminder of YAH's
faithfulness. Thank you for being my cheerleaders even
when you didn't know what you were cheering for.
May you always walk in wisdom, obedience, and abundance.
Mommy loves ya'll forever and always

✦   ✦

To my parents, *Jerome and Vermell* —
thank you for instilling in me the value of hard work and the
power of great faith. Love you much

✦   ✦

To my loving grandmother, *Evelyn* —
thank you for showing me what it truly means to "Keep
YAH First."
At nearly a century of life, your unwavering faith continues
to inspire me.
I love you deeply — keep on praising Him.

Preface

✦   ✦

I was led to write this book because in the midst of making the most money that I had ever made in my life I still found myself lacking financially. At a place where I made six figures each year, I still was waiting for payday to come. It did not make sense. It did not make dollars. It just did not! For one, who has a relationship with God, my financial house was trash.

Faced with debt, bills, and the financial obligations of the breadwinner of my family as a single mother of three, on paper, I had more than enough. BUT my bank account, savings account, and investment account, said something different.

Literally, I woke up one day saying that I needed to change. I needed to exemplify what and who GOD said that I am. That day my tastebuds shifted. I woke up wanting, yearning, desiring, this abundant, whole, heaven on earth, life that I read about in scripture.

I felt embarrassed. I felt disgraced. I felt like a failure. But God.

My God has supplied all of my needs, according to HIS riches and glory by Christ Jesus. There was no doubt that I had Christ

Jesus, but I was lacking in obtaining the ABUNDANT life that Jesus gave us (John 10:10).

I have no doubt that this book will lead you down a path of financial empowerment, faith, enlightenment, and freedom. I pray that the words, from cover to cover, will speak to you right where you are and that you will realize as you engage each chapter that prosperity is your portion. There is nothing too hard for God! Not even your undisciplined ways!

You have the qualities of Prime Stewardship!

Remember, I'm here to empower you to be a good steward over everything that God's blessed you with, that's your faith, family, and finances.

Introduction

✦   ✦

Financial stewardship is more than just budgeting and saving—it is a spiritual discipline that aligns our finances with God's will. The Bible teaches that everything we have belongs to God (Psalm 24:1), and we are called to manage His resources with faithfulness and integrity. This book explores the connection between financial freedom, prayer, and obedience to God's Word, providing a biblical foundation for stewardship that leads to true abundance and peace.

Defining Stewardship

Stewardship means recognizing that we are caretakers, not owners, of our financial resources. Jesus teaches in Luke 16:10, "Whoever can be trusted with very little can also be trusted with much." When we faithfully manage what God entrusts to us—whether little or much—He blesses us with greater opportunities and responsibilities. Prayer and obedience play a crucial role in this process, guiding us to make wise decisions, live within our means, and trust God's provision (Proverbs 3:5-6).

A Promise of Freedom

The world promotes financial security through wealth accumulation, but God offers true financial freedom through trust in Him. "The Lord will open the heavens, the storehouse of his bounty, to send rain on your land in season and to bless all the work of your hands" (Deuteronomy 28:12). When we follow His principles—giving generously (2 Corinthians 9:7), avoiding debt (Proverbs 22:7), and seeking first His kingdom (Matthew 6:33)—we experience freedom from financial stress and walk in His abundant blessings.

Chapter 1: The Foundation of Stewardship

✦   ✦

What is Stewardship?

Stewardship is the biblical principle of managing what God has entrusted to us. The Bible teaches that everything belongs to God, and we are called to wisely and faithfully manage what He provides. Stewardship extends beyond finances; it includes our time, talents, and treasures.

In Genesis 1:26-28, God grants humanity dominion over creation, establishing the first example of stewardship. This role is reaffirmed in Psalm 24:1, which declares, "The earth is the Lord's, and the fullness thereof; the world, and they that dwell therein." Since all belongs to God, our responsibility is to handle His blessings in a way that honors Him.

The Broad Scope of Stewardship

Stewardship is not limited to financial resources. It encompasses how we use our time, how we develop our talents, and how we care for the earth and the people around us. Colossians 3:23 reminds us, "And whatsoever ye do, do it heartily, as to the Lord, and not unto men." Our daily decisions should reflect an awareness of God's ownership over all aspects of our lives. For instance, time is a valuable resource given to us by God. Psalm 90:12 states, "So teach us to number our days, that we may apply our hearts unto wisdom." Properly managing time involves prioritizing prayer, worship, service, and work in ways that align with God's will. Likewise, our talents and skills should be used not for selfish gain but for the edification of others and the glorification of God (1 Peter 4:10).

Ownership vs. Stewardship

A key principle in stewardship is recognizing the difference between ownership and management. The world teaches us to claim possessions as our own, but Scripture reminds us that all we have is given by God. Deuteronomy 8:18 states, "But thou shalt remember the Lord thy God: for it is he that giveth thee power to get wealth, that he may establish his covenant."

When we view our resources as belonging to God, our perspective shifts. We no longer hoard but give generously, recognizing that we are merely channels of His provision. Jesus illustrates this in the Parable of the Talents (Matthew 25:14-30), where the faithful servants managed their master's resources wisely and were rewarded. This parable teaches that God expects us to be diligent and productive with what He has given us, whether it be money, skills, or opportunities.

The Challenge of a Stewardship Mindset

Adopting a stewardship mindset requires a fundamental shift in how we view possessions. Society often promotes materialism and self-reliance, but the Bible calls us to acknowledge God's authority over our lives. When we recognize that our blessings are from Him, we develop humility and gratitude. This shift also changes how we approach giving and generosity. Instead of giving reluctantly, we give joyfully, knowing that we are simply returning what already belongs to God (2 Corinthians 9:7).

Moreover, stewardship involves accountability. Romans 14:12 states, "So then every one of us shall give account of himself to God." One day, we will stand before God and answer for how we have used His resources. This truth should motivate us to live wisely, using our time, finances, and abilities in ways that honor Him.

Scripture as the Guiding Light

God's Word provides clear guidance on how we are to steward our resources. Several key passages highlight the biblical principles of stewardship:

Proverbs 3:9-10 – "Honor the Lord with thy substance, and with the first fruits of all thine increase."
2 Corinthians 9:6-7 – "He which soweth sparingly shall reap also sparingly; and he which soweth bountifully shall reap also bountifully."
Luke 16:10 – "He that is faithful in that which is least is faithful also in much."

These verses emphasize generosity, faithfulness, and the importance of honoring God with what He has given us. Biblical stewardship is a mindset that acknowledges God's ownership and leads us to use His gifts wisely for His kingdom.

Practical Applications of Stewardship

Understanding stewardship is one thing but living it out requires intentional action. Here are some practical ways to apply stewardship in daily life:

1. **Giving and Generosity** – Proverbs 3:9 encourages us to honor God with our substance. Setting aside a portion of income for God's work acknowledges His provision and fosters trust in His continued blessings.

2. **Wise Financial Management** – Avoiding debt, budgeting wisely, and being content with what God has provided are essential principles of stewardship. Hebrews 13:5 warns, "Let your conversation be without covetousness; and be content with such things as ye have."

3. **Time Management** – Prioritizing prayer, worship, service, and family over distractions ensures that we make the most of our God-given time.

4. **Environmental Responsibility** – Caring for the earth reflects an understanding that creation belongs to God. Genesis 2:15 states, "And the Lord God took the man, and put him into the garden of Eden to dress it and to keep it."

5. **Developing Talents for God's Glory** – Whether through music, teaching, leadership, or service, using our skills to benefit others aligns with 1 Peter 4:10.

The Rewards of Faithful Stewardship

Faithful stewardship brings blessings both in this life and the next. Jesus teaches in Luke 6:38, "Give, and it shall be given unto you; good measure, pressed down, and shaken together, and running over." Those who give generously will receive abundantly. Likewise, storing up treasures in heaven (Matthew 6:19-21) ensures that our investments have eternal value.

Ultimately, stewardship is an act of worship. When we live with an awareness that everything belongs to God, we honor Him with our choices and bring glory to His name. As we embrace the role of stewards, we cultivate a heart of gratitude, generosity, and responsibility, seeking to glorify God with all that He has entrusted to us.

Testimony: From Chaos to Clarity

Several years ago, I was buried in credit card debt and felt completely overwhelmed. I began reading scriptures on stewardship and asked God to help me. I started giving faithfully and created a budget. Slowly, things changed. Unexpected opportunities came, and I paid off debt. God honored the obedience and brought peace.

Reflection & Prayer Activity

- **Reflect**: Do you see yourself as an owner or a steward of your resources?

- **Pray**: Ask God to help you shift your mindset and recognize His ownership of everything.

- **Obey**: Choose one financial decision this week to prayerfully submit to God before acting.

A Steward's Surrender

Lord God,

I acknowledge that everything I have—every dollar, every gift, every hour—is from You and belongs to You. Forgive me for the times I have clung to control, claimed ownership, or ignored Your instructions. I surrender my mindset and invite You to transform my thinking.

Make me faithful, wise, and humble in every area You've assigned to me. Teach me to value what You value, to use what I've been given to glorify You and serve others. Let my life reflect the truth that I am a steward, not an owner. Holy Spirit, lead me into greater levels of accountability, intentionality, and honor in all that I manage. In Jesus' name, Amen.

Chapter 2: Trusting God with Your Finances

✦   ✦

Faith in Action

Learning to Trust God in Seasons of Plenty and Lack

Trusting God with our finances is a journey that requires faith, patience, and obedience. It is easy to trust God when there is abundance, but true faith is tested in seasons of lack. The Apostle Paul understood this principle well, stating in Philippians 4:12-13, *"I know what it is to be in need, and I know what it is to have plenty. I have learned the secret of being content in any and every situation, whether well fed or hungry, whether living in plenty or in want. I can do all this through him who gives me strength."* This passage teaches that our financial security does not depend on circumstances but on our unwavering trust in God.

Seasons of financial hardship often reveal where our trust truly lies. Do we rely solely on our jobs, savings, and financial strategies, or do we place our confidence in God's provision? Proverbs 3:5-6 encourages us, *"Trust in the Lord with all your heart and lean not on your own understanding; in all your ways submit to him, and he will make your paths straight."* Financial challenges should lead us to lean on God, seeking His wisdom and guidance rather than panicking or making rash decisions.

Faith in action means continuing to give and manage finances wisely even when resources are limited. Malachi 3:10 assures us of God's faithfulness: *"Bring the whole tithe into the storehouse, that there may be food in my house. Test me in this," says the Lord Almighty, "and see if I will not throw open the floodgates of heaven and pour out so much blessing that there will not be room enough to store it."* Trusting God means believing in His promises and acting accordingly, even when circumstances seem uncertain.

The Role of Prayer

How Prayer Builds Trust and Strengthens Financial Discipline

Prayer is an essential part of trusting God with our finances. Through prayer, we acknowledge God as the ultimate provider and invite Him into our financial decisions. Philippians 4:6-7 encourages us: *"Do not be anxious about anything, but in every situation, by prayer and petition, with thanksgiving, present your requests to God. And the peace of God, which transcends all understanding, will guard your hearts and your minds in Christ Jesus."* When we pray about our financial concerns, God replaces anxiety with peace and direction.

Financial discipline is a crucial aspect of stewardship, and prayer helps align our financial habits with God's wisdom. James 1:5 tells us, *"If any of you lacks wisdom, you should ask God, who gives generously to all without finding fault, and it will be given to you."* Before making major financial decisions—such as taking on debt, making investments, or starting a business—believers should seek God's guidance in prayer. When we rely on His wisdom rather than our own, we often avoid financial pitfalls and make sound, faith-driven choices.

Another aspect of financial prayer is gratitude. 1 Thessalonians 5:16-18 commands us to *"Rejoice always, pray continually, give thanks in all circumstances; for this is God's will for you in Christ Jesus."* Gratitude keeps our focus on God's blessings rather than financial worries. By continually thanking God for His provision, we develop a heart of contentment, which is key to financial peace.

Walking in Financial Trust

Trusting God with our finances is a lifelong journey of faith, obedience, and prayer. Whether in times of plenty or lack, we are called to rely on God as our provider. Faith in action means continuing to trust God even when financial situations seem dire.

Through prayer, we build a deeper reliance on Him, allowing Him to shape our financial habits and decisions.

God's faithfulness is evident throughout Scripture and in the lives of those who trust Him. Matthew 6:31-33 reassures us: *"So do not worry, saying, 'What shall we eat?' or 'What shall we drink?' or 'What shall we wear?' For the pagans run after all these things, and your heavenly Father knows that you need them. But seek first his kingdom and his righteousness, and all these things will be given to you as well."* When we put God first in our finances and trust Him fully, He meets our needs in ways beyond our understanding.

The testimonies of God's provision remind us that He is always faithful. By seeking His kingdom first, practicing gratitude, and acting in faith, we experience the true financial freedom that comes from trusting in Him. Proverbs 16:3 encourages us, *"Commit to the Lord whatever you do, and he will establish your plans."* When we commit our finances to God, He leads us to peace, provision, and prosperity in His perfect timing.

Testimony: Daily Bread

When I lost my job, fear set in. But I prayed, gave my time, my talent and when I had funds; I gave my treasures to Kingdom work, and trusted God. I found multiple opportunities that assisted with everything from food to mortgage payments for over a year and regardless of my employment status in the future.

God taught me that He really does provide our daily bread when we trust Him.

Reflection & Prayer Activity

- **Reflect**: Where do you find it hardest to trust God financially?

- **Pray**: Ask God to build your faith in His provision and give you peace.

- **Obey**: Step out in faith by giving or tithing, even if it's small. Trust Him with the result.

Trusting the Hand I Cannot See

Father in Heaven,

You are my Rock and my Provider. When my eyes see lack, help my heart remember Your abundance. When I'm tempted to worry or panic, anchor me in Your promises. Strengthen my trust, even when I don't understand the path ahead.

Help me to make faith-led decisions, not fear-based reactions. Give me boldness to give, patience to wait, and wisdom to manage what You've entrusted to me. May my finances be a reflection of my faith—not just in what I do, but in how I trust.

I choose today to trust the hand I cannot see, knowing You are always working for my good. In Jesus' name, Amen.

Chapter 3: Obedience Brings Blessings

✦   ✦

The Call to Obey

Understanding God's Commands about Giving, and Stewardship

Obedience to God is a cornerstone of the Christian life, especially in the area of financial stewardship. The Bible is clear that God desires obedience more than sacrifice (1 Samuel 15:22), and this includes how we handle our money. Deuteronomy 28:1-2 says, *"If you fully obey the Lord your God and carefully follow all his commands I give you today, the Lord your God will set you high above all the nations on earth. All these blessings will come on you and accompany you if you obey the Lord your God."* Obedience positions us to receive God's blessings.

Monetary giving is one of the ways we demonstrate obedience and honor God with our finances. In the New Testament, giving is not presented as a rigid law but as a reflection of our love, generosity, and trust in God's provision. Paul reminds us in 2 Corinthians 9:7 that "each of you should give what you have decided in your heart to give, not reluctantly or under compulsion, for God loves a cheerful giver."

Giving is not about meeting a legal requirement; it's about surrender and worship. When we freely give, we acknowledge that everything we have belongs to God, and we are simply stewards of His resources. Our generosity fuels kingdom work, meets the needs of others, and opens the door for God's blessings to overflow in our lives.

Proverbs 19:17 declares, "Whoever is kind to the poor lends to the Lord, and He will reward them for what they have done." Likewise, Proverbs 28:27 reminds us, "Those who give to the poor will lack nothing, but those who close their eyes to them receive many curses." When we give to the poor and care for those in need, we are reflecting God's heart and participating in His promise of provision.

Generosity is another command that reflects obedience. Proverbs 11:25 declares, *"A generous person will prosper; whoever refreshes others will be refreshed."* Obedience to God often requires us to give even when it's uncomfortable or inconvenient. Yet, it's in those moments that God reveals His faithfulness and provision.

The Blessing of Generosity
How Obedience Opens the Door to God's Provision

When we obey God with a generous heart, we activate the principles of sowing and reaping. 2 Corinthians 9:6-8 states, *"Remember this: Whoever sows sparingly will also reap sparingly, and whoever sows generously will also reap generously. Each of you should give what you have decided in your heart to give, not reluctantly or under compulsion, for God loves a cheerful giver. And God is able to bless you abundantly, so that in all things at all times, having all that you need, you will abound in every good work."*

Obedience and generosity go hand in hand. God doesn't just bless us so we can be comfortable; He blesses us so we can be a blessing to others. When we give in obedience to God, whether through offerings, or charitable deeds, we reflect His character. Luke 6:38 promises, *"Give, and it will be given to you. A good measure, pressed down, shaken together and running over, will be poured into your lap. For with the measure you use, it will be measured to you."*

There is also protection in obedience. When we follow God's financial principles, we are shielded from many of the pitfalls that trap others—debt, greed, impulsive spending. Psalm 37:25 says,

"I was young and now I am old, yet I have never seen the righteous forsaken or their children begging bread." Righteousness and obedience often go hand in hand; when we live according to God's Word, He ensures we are taken care of.

Overcoming Challenges to Obedience

Fear, Doubt, and Practical Steps to Trust God Fully

Despite the clear promises of God, many believers struggle to walk in obedience with their finances. Fear is one of the biggest barriers. The thought of giving sacrificially can be daunting when bills are piling up or income is uncertain. But God calls us to walk by faith, not by sight (2 Corinthians 5:7).

One way to overcome fear is through the Word of God. Romans 10:17 reminds us, *"Faith comes from hearing the message, and the message is heard through the word about Christ."* Immersing ourselves in God's promises builds the faith needed to obey Him, even when it's hard.

Doubt is another challenge. We may wonder if obedience really leads to blessings, especially when we don't see immediate results. But Galatians 6:9 encourages us, *"Let us not become weary in doing good, for at the proper time we will reap a harvest if we do not give up."* Obedience is often a long-term investment, not a quick fix.

Trusting God means believing He is working even when we don't see it.

Practical steps to develop obedience include:

1. **Start small**: If giving in monetary ways seems overwhelming, start with a consistent percentage and grow from there.

2. **Create a budget**: Stewardship begins with knowing where your money goes.

3. **Pray for strength and wisdom**: Ask God daily to help you obey Him.

4. **Find accountability**: Share your goals with a trusted mentor or friend.

Choosing Obedience in Every Season

Obedience is not always easy, but it is always rewarding. In finances, as in every area of life, God honors those who honor Him. 1 Kings 2:3 tells us, *"Observe what the Lord your God requires: Walk in obedience to Him, and keep His decrees and commands...so that you may prosper in all you do and wherever you go."* Financial obedience is an act of worship, a declaration that we trust God more than we trust money.

No matter what season you're in—plenty or lack—choose obedience. Obey by giving, budgeting, and seeking God's wisdom. Stand on His promises, and watch how He faithfully provides, protects, and prospers.

Testimony: A Risk that Paid Off

A friend once gave her last $50 to a missionary. That same day, she received $500 unexpectedly. Her act of obedience became a faith anchor. God used it to not only show His goodness but to build her faith even more.

Reflection & Prayer Activity

- **Reflect**: Is fear keeping you from obeying God in your finances?

- **Pray**: Ask God to give you courage to follow His instructions.

- **Obey**: Take one specific, obedient step this week, like, forgiving a debt, or helping someone in need.

Obedience that Unlocks Overflow

Lord,

You are worthy of my full obedience. I confess the times I delayed, doubted, or dismissed Your instructions. Today, I choose to obey—not out of obligation, but out of love and trust. You have never failed me, and I believe that my obedience opens the door to Your provision.

Even when it's uncomfortable, stretch me to give generously. Even when it doesn't make sense, teach me to respond quickly and cheerfully. Remind me that my sacrifice is never wasted in Your Kingdom.

Let my life be marked by consistent, joyful obedience—because I know that where You lead, blessings follow. In Jesus' name, Amen.

Chapter 4: Developing a Stewardship Mindset

✦   ✦

Setting Godly Financial Goals

Aligning Your Plans with God's Will

True stewardship begins with purpose. When our financial goals are rooted in God's will, they become tools for advancing His kingdom rather than just serving our desires. Proverbs 16:3 says, "Commit to the Lord whatever you do, and he will establish your plans." Financial goals, whether for saving, giving, or investing, should begin with prayerful consideration of what honors God.

James 4:13-15 reminds us of the importance of seeking God's direction: "You who say, 'Today or tomorrow we will go to this or that city, spend a year there, carry on business and make money.' Why, you do not even know what will happen tomorrow... Instead, you ought to say, 'If it is the Lord's will, we will live and do this or that.'" This scripture challenges us to be humble in our financial planning and to consult the Father for direction.

Contentment and Gratitude
Breaking Free from the Culture of Materialism

In a world that constantly pushes us to accumulate more, stewardship requires a countercultural mindset. Contentment is a spiritual posture that acknowledges God's sufficiency. 1 Timothy 6:6-8 states, "But godliness with contentment is great gain. For we brought nothing into the world, and we can take nothing out of it."

Hebrews 13:5 reinforces this truth: "Keep your lives free from the love of money and be content with what you have, because God has said, 'Never will I leave you; never will I forsake you.'" When we cultivate gratitude, we shift our focus from what we lack to what we've been given. This shift is key to sustaining a stewardship mindset.

One simple practice to cultivate contentment is to begin each day by listing three things you are grateful for. When our hearts are filled with thanksgiving, there is less room for comparison or greed.

Practical Budgeting as Worship
Viewing Your Financial Planning as an Act of Obedience

Budgeting may seem like a mundane task, but when approached with the right heart, it becomes an act of worship. It reflects discipline, planning, and care for what God has entrusted to us. Luke 14:28 illustrates this principle: "Suppose one of you wants to build a tower. Won't you first sit down and estimate the cost to see if you have enough money to complete it?"

Creating and following a budget is not about restriction—it's about intention. It allows us to prioritize giving, avoid unnecessary debt, and steward well the resources we've been given. Proverbs 21:5 reminds us, "The plans of the diligent lead to profit as surely as haste leads to poverty."

When budgeting is done prayerfully and with God's guidance, it becomes a spiritual discipline that keeps our hearts aligned with His will. Allocate your resources as a form of honor: give first, save wisely, and spend prayerfully.

Testimony: From Chaos to Clarity

There was a season when I lived paycheck to paycheck with no clear direction. Once I began involving God in my financial goals, practicing contentment, and creating a budget, everything shifted.

I gained peace, began giving consistently, and even started saving. God didn't just change my finances—He changed my mindset.

Reflection & Prayer Activity

- **Reflect**: Are your current financial goals aligned with God's purpose for your life?

- **Pray**: Ask God to show you how to honor Him with your financial goals and day-to-day decisions.

- **Obey**: Create or review your budget this week, dedicating it to God. Start with a prayer and prioritize giving.

A Mindset Anchored in Heaven

Father,

Renew my mind. Transform the way I think about money, goals, and success. Strip away every worldly definition and replace it with Your truth. May I never chase what doesn't satisfy, but instead seek the things that please Your heart. Help me to live with holy contentment, godly ambition, and clear vision. Teach me to budget with worship, to give with joy, and to plan with purpose. Let my financial mindset reflect heaven's perspective. Today, I release the pressure to perform and embrace the peace of being aligned with You. In all I do, be glorified. In Jesus' name, Amen.

Chapter 5: Prayer as Your Financial Compass

✦   ✦

Praying with Purpose

Seeking God's Wisdom in Financial Decisions

Prayer is not a last resort—it is the believer's first response. When we treat prayer as a compass, we navigate life with divine direction, including in our finances. James 1:5 assures us, "If any of you lacks wisdom, you should ask God, who gives generously to all without finding fault, and it will be given to you." Every financial decision—whether major or minor—should be filtered through the lens of prayer.

Before making decisions about a job offer, an investment, or a large purchase, stop and ask God for His insight. Proverbs 3:6 encourages, "In all your ways acknowledge Him, and He will make your paths straight." When we involve God early in the process, we avoid costly mistakes and align our choices with His will.

Listening to God's Guidance
Discernment in Investments, Spending, and Giving

Prayer is a two-way conversation. After presenting our requests, we must make space to listen. God may respond through scripture, godly counsel, peace or unrest in our spirit, or unexpected doors opening—or closing.

John 10:27 says, "My sheep listen to my voice; I know them, and they follow me." The more we practice stillness before God, the more sensitive we become to His leading. Listening is crucial in discerning the timing and direction of financial decisions.

God may tell you to wait when you're ready to act, or to give when you'd rather hold back. Sometimes His answers don't make immediate sense, but they always carry eternal value. My advice is to **OBEY IMMEDIATELY**!

Creating a Habit of Prayerful Stewardship

Daily Practices to Stay Aligned

Developing a prayer habit builds spiritual awareness and financial resilience. Daniel prayed three times a day (Daniel 6:10), showing that regular communion with God is vital for staying on course.

Incorporate financial prayer into your daily routine:

- Begin your day asking for wisdom and provision.

- Pray over your budget weekly.

- Give thanks for every financial blessing.

- Intercede for others' financial needs.

1 Thessalonians 5:17 encourages us to "pray without ceasing." While this doesn't mean constant talking, it does mean maintaining an ongoing awareness of and dependence on God throughout the day. Prayer is not just an emergency tool—it's a lifestyle.

Testimony
A Prayer-Guided Purchase

I purchased a car out of a need and did not consult God about it at all. The purchase went so smoothly I was easily approved, I could afford the payments, and I needed a car. I had the car for about a year before I ran into trouble affording the car, and it was at this time that I made a major decision to do a voluntary repossession. It was also at this time that I consulted God on a new car. After much prayer, God told me to apply for a loan and eight months after the repossession, I was approved to purchase a brand-new vehicle. That experience taught me to never underestimate the power of a pause in prayer. God's way is always better.

Reflection & Prayer Activity

- **Reflect**: Do you invite God into your financial decisions before acting or only after trouble comes?

- **Pray**: Ask God for the discipline to seek Him first and the sensitivity to hear His voice.

- **Obey**: This week, take one financial decision—big or small—and submit it to God in prayer. Journal what you sense He's saying.

Led by Your Voice, Not by My Wallet

Holy Spirit,

Be my compass. Let Your voice guide me through every financial decision I face. Tune my ears to hear You clearly, and give me the courage to follow— even when it costs, even when it stretches, even when it's slow.

I no longer want to be led by money, pressure, or fear. I want to be led by You. Interrupt my plans if they don't align with Your will. Redirect me when I wander. Confirm my steps with peace and provision.

I declare that You are Lord over my finances—not just in word, but in action. In Jesus' name, Amen.

Chapter 6: Overcoming Financial Strongholds

✦   ✦

Identifying Spiritual Roadblocks

Pride, Greed, Fear, and Other Barriers to Freedom

Financial strongholds are more than habits—they are spiritual hindrances that block us from living in the abundance God has for us. These strongholds often manifest as pride, greed, fear, laziness, or a scarcity mindset. 2 Corinthians 10:4-5 reminds us, *"The weapons we fight with are not the weapons of the world. On the contrary, they have divine power to demolish strongholds."*

Pride says, "I earned this, I control this." But Deuteronomy 8:18 says, *"But remember the Lord your God, for it is he who gives you the ability to produce wealth."* Greed whispers, "You need more to feel secure." Fear screams, "There's never enough." These mindsets must be torn down through truth and surrender.

Ask yourself: What thought patterns govern my financial behavior? Are they rooted in faith or fear? Trust or control? Identifying the root is the first step to freedom.

Breaking Free Through Prayer
Strategies for Spiritual and Financial Breakthroughs

Freedom begins with confession and intercession. 1 John 1:9 says, *"If we confess our sins, He is faithful and just and will forgive us our sins and purify us from all unrighteousness."* Start by bringing your financial strongholds before God in prayer. Renounce them. Declare your dependence on Him.

Use scriptures in your warfare. For example:

- **Against fear**: *"My God will supply all my needs"* (Philippians 4:19).

- **Against greed**: *"Life does not consist in the abundance of possessions"* (Luke 12:15).

- **Against pride**: *"Humble yourselves before the Lord, and He will lift you up"* (James 4:10).

Fasting can also be a powerful tool. Isaiah 58:6 says, *"Is not this the kind of fasting I have chosen: to loose the chains of injustice and untie the cords of the yoke...?"* Fasting, paired with prayer, sharpens our spiritual discernment and breaks strongholds.

The Power of Forgiveness
Letting Go of Debt, Grudges, and Self-Condemnation

Unforgiveness—whether toward others or ourselves—can block financial breakthrough. Holding on to past financial failures, mistakes, or debts (emotional or monetary) weighs us down.

Ephesians 4:31-32 urges us to *"Get rid of all bitterness, rage and anger...Be kind and compassionate to one another, forgiving each other, just as in Christ God forgave you."* Sometimes the greatest financial freedom comes when we forgive a borrower, a business partner, or ourselves.

Romans 8:1 reminds us, *"Therefore, there is now no condemnation for those who are in Christ Jesus."* If you've mismanaged money or made poor decisions, confess it, receive grace, and move forward. You are not disqualified from God's blessings.

Testimony: Letting Go of Control

A young professional shared that her breakthrough came only after she released her obsession with control. She always feared losing everything, so she hoarded and never gave. Through prayer, she confessed her fear and committed to giving to the poor. That small act of obedience cracked the stronghold. Peace replaced anxiety, and doors began to open financially and spiritually.

Reflection & Prayer Activity

- **Reflect**: What spiritual stronghold has had the greatest grip on your finances—pride, fear, greed, or something else?

- **Pray**: Ask God to expose and demolish any strongholds in your financial mindset. Speak scriptures that counter those lies.

- **Obey**: Choose one action to symbolically break free—, give generously to the poor, forgive a debt, or journal your confession.

Freedom Over My Finances

Lord God,

I come against every lie that has kept me in bondage—every mindset of lack, fear, pride, or control. I renounce every stronghold that says, "I'll never get ahead," or "I have to do it on my own."

By Your power, I declare freedom. I am no longer a slave to past mistakes or current limitations. You are tearing down walls, lifting burdens, and leading me into wholeness. Give me strength to forgive, discipline to change, and

courage to believe again. Where the Spirit of the Lord is, there is liberty—
and I receive that liberty now. In Jesus' name, Amen.

Chapter 7: Living in Financial Freedom

✦   ✦

Redefining Success

What True Financial Freedom Looks Like in God's Eyes

The world defines success by accumulation—more money, more assets, more influence. But God defines success by stewardship—how well we manage what He gives us. Luke 12:15 reminds us, *"Life does not consist in an abundance of possessions."* True financial freedom is living with peace, purpose, and the ability to bless others.

When we live debt-free, give generously, and have margin in our finances, we're free to serve God fully. Galatians 5:1 says, *"It is for freedom that Christ has set us free."* Financial freedom allows us to respond to God's call without hesitation or constraint.

A Life of Generosity and Purpose

Using Your Resources to Serve and Bless Others

When we shift from consuming to contributing, our finances become a vehicle for ministry. 1 Peter 4:10 encourages us, *"Each of you should use whatever gift you have received to serve others, as faithful stewards of God's grace in its various forms."* This includes financial gifts.

Ask yourself: How can I use what God has given me to bless my church, community, and family? Whether it's supporting a missionary, helping someone in need, or investing in Kingdom work, generosity is the natural fruit of a faithful steward.

Sustaining Freedom

Building a Legacy of Stewardship for Future Generations

Stewardship doesn't stop with us—it's something we model and pass on. Proverbs 13:22 says, *"A good person leaves an inheritance for their children's children."* That inheritance isn't just financial—it's spiritual. We are called to disciple our children and others in the principles of stewardship.

Talk about giving and budgeting with your family. Show them how you honor God with your money. Create a legacy not just of wealth but of wisdom.

The Joy of Walking in God's Plan

A Renewed Vision

Reflecting on the Journey of Prayer and Obedience

As you close the final chapter of this book, take a moment to reflect on the journey you've walked through. From learning the foundational truths of stewardship to experiencing the transformational power of prayer and obedience, you now carry a renewed vision of what it means to honor God with your finances. This is more than budgeting or giving—it's a heart posture. It's a lifestyle of surrender and trust. Through every scripture, testimony, and prayer, you've been invited into deeper intimacy with YAH as your Provider, Shepherd, and Father.

Encouragement to Stay Faithful

Continuing to Grow as a Steward of God's Gifts

The road to financial freedom is not without challenges, but it is filled with purpose. Stay the course. Stewardship is not a one-time act—it's a daily commitment to walk in obedience and trust. Don't be discouraged by setbacks or delays. Galatians 6:9 reminds us, *"Let us not grow weary in doing good, for at the proper time we will reap a harvest if we do not give up."* Continue to seek God's wisdom, live generously, and cultivate contentment. You are not alone—He is with you every step of the way.

A Call to Action:

- **Pray daily** for wisdom and direction over your finances.

- **Review your budget** monthly with God at the center.

- **Give as God directs**, trusting that obedience brings blessing.

- **Teach others** what you've learned—whether your children, spouse, or community.

- **Set financial goals** that align with God's purpose for your life.

- **Stay connected** to a community of faith-filled stewards for encouragement and accountability.

You've been equipped to walk in freedom. Now walk it out with boldness and joy. God delights in faithful stewards, and as you continue to obey, He will continue to provide, guide, and multiply. This is the joy of walking in His plan.

Testimony: A Family Transformed

One family began practicing biblical stewardship together. They created a giving jar, started praying over their budget, and included their children in the process. Over time, not only did their finances improve—but their family culture changed. Joy and unity replaced stress and tension.

Reflection & Prayer Activity

- **Reflect**: What does financial freedom mean to you today? Is your definition aligned with scripture?

- **Pray**: Ask God for a vision of the legacy He wants you to build through your finances.

- **Obey**: Begin planning one step to teach or model stewardship for someone else.

Walking Boldly in Financial Freedom

Father,

Thank You for inviting me into a life of freedom—a life not bound by fear, debt, or worldly pressure. I walk in Your provision, Your peace, and Your purpose. Let this freedom not just bless me, but flow through me to others.

Make me a vessel of generosity, a testimony of stewardship, and a model of Your grace. I don't want temporary wealth—I want eternal impact.

Establish my legacy. Bless my household. And let every financial decision from this day forward honor Your name. I walk boldly, because I walk with You. In Jesus' name, Amen.

"Well done, good and faithful servant." – Matthew 25:21

Bonus Section

✦   ✦

Speak these declarations daily to build your faith, renew your mind, and align your heart with God's promises regarding provision, wisdom, and stewardship.

1. **God is my source and provider; I shall not lack. (Philippians 4:19)**
2. **The Lord gives me the ability to produce wealth. (Deuteronomy 8:18)**
3. **I honor the Lord with my wealth, and my barns are filled. (Proverbs 3:9-10)**
4. **I am a cheerful giver and God blesses me abundantly. (2 Corinthians 9:7-8)**
5. **I lend and do not borrow; I am the head and not the tail. (Deuteronomy 28:12-13)**
6. **I seek first God's Kingdom, and all things are added to me. (Matthew 6:33)**
7. **I do not worry about money because God takes care of me. (Matthew 6:31-32)**

8. I walk in wisdom regarding all financial matters. (James 1:5)

9. I have peace in my finances because I trust in God. (Isaiah 26:3)

10. The Lord teaches me to profit and leads me in the way I should go. (Isaiah 48:17)

11. I am faithful with little and God entrusts me with more. (Luke 16:10)

12. I live in contentment and godliness, which is great gain. (1 Timothy 6:6)

13. My generosity opens doors and brings increase. (Proverbs 11:25)

14. I owe no man anything but love. (Romans 13:8)

15. I have the discipline to budget and steward well. (Proverbs 21:5)

16. The Lord delights in my obedience with finances. (1 Samuel 15:22)

17. I break every spirit of fear and walk in God's perfect provision. (2 Timothy 1:7)

18. I am blessed to be a blessing to others. (Genesis 12:2)

19. I forgive financial wrongs and walk in freedom. (Ephesians 4:31-32)

20. I am not anxious because I present every need to God in prayer.(Philippians 4:6-7)

21. I fast and pray for financial clarity and direction. (Isaiah 58:6)

22. My faith activates God's provision in every season. (Hebrews 11:6)

23. I walk in integrity in all financial dealings. (Proverbs 10:9)

24. God makes all grace abound toward me in every way. (2 Corinthians 9:8)

25. I store up treasure in heaven by giving on earth. (Matthew 6:20-21)

26. I avoid the love of money and pursue righteousness. (1 Timothy 6:10-11)

27. The blessing of the Lord makes me rich and adds no sorrow. (Proverbs 10:22)

28. I trust in God, not in riches. (1 Timothy 6:17)

29. I rejoice in God's daily provision and give thanks always. (1 Thessalonians 5:18)

30. I walk in divine financial alignment and favor all the days of my life. (Psalm 23:1,6)

Speak them!

Believe them!

Live them!

Connect With Shamika Patrice

Thank you for walking this journey of faith and financial freedom with me! My prayer is that *Stewardship: Financial Freedom through Prayer and Obedience* has encouraged you to trust God with every area of your life — especially your finances.

This isn't the end; it's the beginning of a lifestyle rooted in obedience, abundance, and purpose. I'd love to stay connected and help you continue your journey toward becoming the faithful steward God designed you to be.

Website: www.PrimeStewardship.com

Email: srivers@smjdenterprises.com

Instagram: @PrimeStewardship

Get Free Resources:

Visit **PrimeStewardship.com** to download your *7-Day Stewardship Plan*, access financial devotionals, and explore workshops and coaching opportunities designed to strengthen your faith, family, and finances.

Share Your Testimony: Has this book blessed you? I'd love to hear from you! Tag your post or message with **#PrimeStewardship** to inspire others walking the same journey.

Together, we're building a community of believers who choose obedience over anxiety, stewardship over struggle, and faith over fear.

Let's keep growing, giving, and glorifying God — one act of stewardship at a time.